FOOD & FEASTS

in

Tudor Times

Richard Balkwill

Parsippany, New Jersey

First American publication 1995 by New Discovery Books, an imprint of Silver Burdett Press.
A Simon & Schuster Company
299 Jefferson Road, Parsippany, NJ 07054

First published in 1995 in Great Britain by
Wayland (Publishers) Ltd

A ZOË BOOK

Copyright © 1995 Zoë Books Limited

Devised and produced by
Zoë Books Limited
15 Worthy Lane
Winchester
Hampshire SO23 7AB
England

Printed in Italy by Grafedit SpA.
Design: Jan Sterling, Sterling Associates
Picture research: Victoria Sturgess
Maps: Gecko Limited
Production: Grahame Griffiths

10 9 8 7 6 5 4 3 2 1

Library of Congress Cataloging-in-Publication Data

Balkwill, Richard.
    Food & feasts in Tudor times / Richard Balkwill.
        p. cm.—(Food & feasts)
    Includes bibliographical references and index.
    ISBN 0-02-726319-3
    1. Food habits—England—History—16th century—
Juvenile Literature. 2. England—Social life and customs—
Juvenile literature. [1. Food habits—Europe—History.
2. Europe—Social life and customs—16th century.
3. Cookery, European.]. I. Title. II. Title: Food and feasts
in Tudor times. III. Series.
GT2853.G7B35   1995
394.1'2'094209031—dc20   94-26500

Summary: A social history of the Tudor period in England, explaining what foods were eaten and how they were prepared; emphasizes the kinds of food eaten by country people, townspeople, nobility, and royalty, and the new foods available as a result of increased travel.

Photographic acknowledgments

The publishers wish to acknowledge, with thanks, the following photographic sources:

Ancient Art & Architecture Collection 3,25r; Bibliothèque Nationale, Paris 11b,23b; The Bridgeman Art Library 5b,11t / British Library 6 / British Museum 24 / Giraudon title page / Kunsthistorisches Museum, Vienna 12,17 / Phillips 14; The British Library, London 16b,19,21t; Mary Evans Picture Library 5t,8r,9b,21b,22; The Feathers Hotel, Ludlow 23t; Glasgow Museums, The Burrell Collection 8l; Department of Printing & Graphic Arts, The Houghton Library, Harvard University 10,13b; Louvre, Paris © photo R.M.N. 9r; courtesy of The Marquess of Salisbury 18; courtesy of Museum of Fine Arts, Boston 7bl&r,16t; National Gallery of Scotland 25l; Roger-Viollet / Boyer 13t; The Royal Collection © 1994 Her Majesty Queen Elizabeth II 15t,20; The Board of the Trustees of the Victoria & Albert Museum 15b; The Warburg Institute, University of London 7t.

Cover: The Bridgeman Art Library / British Library center / Giraudon bottom; Mary Evans Picture Library top left & right

The publishers have made every effort to trace the copyright holders, but if they have inadvertently overlooked any, they will be pleased to make the necessary arrangement at the first opportunity.

Contents

Introduction

A Welshman named Owen Tudor, who died in 1461, gave the Tudor period its name. His grandson Henry Tudor founded the Tudor ruling family, or **dynasty**, which lasted from 1485 until 1603. Henry became King Henry VII in 1485, after winning the Battle of Bosworth. Other Tudor **monarchs** were Henry VIII, Edward VI, Mary I, and Elizabeth I.

The kings and queens of England at this time ruled a country with a tiny, scattered population. There were fewer than 5 million people, compared with today's 56 million. Towns were small. No city in England or Wales had a population of more than 200,000. Venice and Paris were bigger than London.

In Europe and in the rest of the world, great changes took place between 1500 to 1600. Explorers traveled by sea to parts of the world not known to many Europeans. Christopher Columbus landed in what is now the Americas in 1492, while Vasco da Gama reached India. In 1522 the expedition led by Magellan was the first to sail around the world.

Sir Francis Drake also sailed around the world. In 1577 he returned to England with gold and silver from the Caribbean

Kings and Queens of England

Henry VII, 1485-1509
Henry VIII, 1509-1547
Edward VI, 1547-1553
Mary I, 1553-1558
Elizabeth I, 1558-1603

Kings of France

Charles VIII, 1483-1498
Louis XII, 1498-1515
François I, 1515-1547
Henri II, 1547-1559
François II, 1559-1560
Charles IX, 1560-1574
Henri III, 1574-1589
Henri IV, 1589-1610

Holy Roman Empire

Charles V, 1519-1556

Spain

Philip II, 1556-1598

▽ The main voyages of discovery and Europe in Tudor times

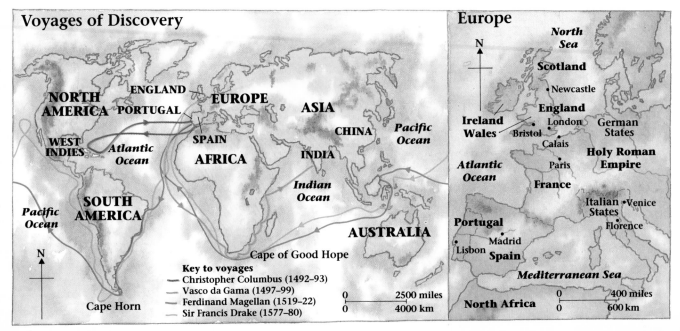

Voyages of Discovery

NORTH AMERICA
ENGLAND
PORTUGAL
EUROPE
ASIA
CHINA
Pacific Ocean
WEST INDIES
Atlantic Ocean
SPAIN
AFRICA
INDIA
SOUTH AMERICA
Pacific Ocean
Indian Ocean
AUSTRALIA
Cape of Good Hope
Cape Horn
N

Key to voyages
— Christopher Columbus (1492–93)
— Vasco da Gama (1497–99)
— Ferdinand Magellan (1519–22)
— Sir Francis Drake (1577–80)

0   2500 miles
0   4000 km

Europe

North Sea
N
Scotland
• Newcastle
Ireland
England
Wales
• London
German States
Bristol •
Calais
Holy Roman Empire
Atlantic Ocean
Paris
France
Italian States
• Venice
Florence
Portugal
• Madrid
Lisbon • Spain
Mediterranean Sea
North Africa

0   400 miles
0   600 km

△ This woodcut shows an Italian kitchen. It is from a cookbook by Christoforo di Messisburgo that was published in Ferrara, Italy, in 1549.

Dough is being rolled out on the left. Two assistants are turning the **spits**. A rather tiny man is fanning the fire with a pair of bellows. Joints of meat and birds have been prepared. The dog has a bone to chew.

One of the earliest printed recipe books was written in French by Lancelot de Casteau. It was called *Ouverture de Cuisine* (Introduction to Cookery) and was published in 1604.

and Mexico, as well as spices such as ginger and pepper. Sir Walter Raleigh brought new foods, such as maize (or corn) and potatoes, from the New World. He also introduced tobacco, which was thought to be a cure for illness.

Travel by land was slow and difficult. But in Europe, wealth and knowledge were increasing. In Italy, people began to be interested in the arts and sciences of ancient Greece and Rome. They studied the medicine, mathematics, literature, sculpture, and buildings of the ancient world. This movement, known as the **Renaissance** (or "rebirth"), spread across Europe.

The invention of the printing press made it easier for ideas and information to be exchanged. People were able to read about what happened in other countries, as well as about the ways of life, or lifestyles, of different peoples. It was possible to read about food in other parts of the world, too, from the recipe books that were printed at about this time.

▽ *Summer* by Arcimboldo, 1563. This painting seems to be a picture of freshly picked summer fruits and vegetables. But look more closely and you will also see a man sitting and looking up to the left. His hair is made of grapes, his cheeks are mushrooms, his arms are celery, and his legs and feet are maize and turnips.

Farming and food in the countryside

The kind of food eaten by people in Tudor times depended on the type of family into which a person was born. There were huge differences between the lives of rich and poor people. Rich people ate a wide variety of food, including plenty of meat and fish. Feasts or **banquets** were often held at the ruler's court. Meanwhile, in the countryside, poor people ate whatever they could grow or raise on land that did not belong to them, in a climate that was often wet and cold.

The summers of 1594, 1595, 1596, and 1597 were cold and wet. Crops could not be harvested, and they rotted in the fields. This led to food shortages, or **famine**, and riots.

Life on the land

For hundreds of years, people in the country-side had lived under the **feudal** system. The landowner, who lived in a castle or **manor**

▷ This illustration of "plowing, sowing, and harrowing" comes from an English book made in 1520.

In the background two horses are pulling a plow. The man with a whip is driving a horse-drawn **harrow**, used to break up and flatten the earth. Someone else is sowing seeds by scattering, or **broadcasting**, them. All these activities would not take place at the same time; the painter is trying to show the details together in one picture.

▷ This country scene was engraved by Jacob Matham in 1603. It was based on a picture by the Dutch painter Pieter Aertens. There are baskets of fresh fruit and vegetables, and there are eggs and a cockerel, or male chicken. In the background, farm workers are resting.

house, controlled all the land in an area. Farmers worked in the owner's fields, and also on small pieces of land where they grew food for their own families. Cattle, sheep, and horses were owned by wealthy people, while the poor tenants might keep a pig or two. Poor people were allowed to graze their animals on common land.

This system was slowly changing in England and Wales in Tudor times. In some areas, landowners began to keep more sheep and to grow fewer crops. Instead of working on the

▽ These pictures are from *The Twelve Months*, by Virgil Solis. They show winter work in the countryside. In "November," pigs are fattened on acorns, and cattle are killed.

▽ In "December," pigs are killed, and the meat is prepared for cooking. The hams are being put to soak in salted water, or **brine**.

owner's land, the tenants paid rent for their small plots. The changes brought problems when some open fields were fenced in, or **enclosed**, and poorer people had nowhere to grow food.

Food for land workers

The most important food for country people was a thick soup, or **pottage**. It was made with vegetables such as cabbage and beans and was thickened with oatmeal or barley. Sometimes meat might be added. Root vegetables such as turnips were grown, but potatoes were not known until later in the Tudor period. People ate salads made of onions, radishes, garlic, and cucumber, as well as lettuce. Tomatoes were also unknown.

Most villages had their own bakers. The oven was heated, and mounds of dough were put into it. Then the oven door was sealed up with mud. A skilled baker knew exactly when to break open the door and remove the cooked bread.

Bread was usually made into buns, rather than loaves. The best-quality bread was called manchet, and the less good was called cheat. People used a flat wedge of bread or a trencher as a mat or plate. Juices from the food they ate would soak into the bread. Sometimes the used trenchers were given to poor people.

For the worker in the country, meat was a rare treat on feast days. An ox, a sheep, or a pig might be roasted by turning it on a spike or spit over an open fire. Pork from pigs was

William Harrison wrote in his *Description of England*, published in 1577, that when times were hard, people had to content themselves with, "bread made of beans, peas or oats, or all together, and some acorns too."

▽ This 16th-century German picture shows the killing of a wild boar for the kitchen, while someone else is chopping down a tree. It is hard to tell why the man on the right has been put in the **stocks**.

▽ These pictures, called *The Bakers of York* were drawn in 1595. You can see a couple checking grain or flour, another person kneading dough, followed by others baking and selling the bread. The words over the top encourage the baker to do his job well!

usually salted or smoked to make ham and bacon. It was **preserved** in this way to prevent it from spoiling. Meat such as mutton from sheep and venison from deer was eaten by richer people.

No one was allowed to eat meat on Fridays. On this day, people ate fish. It usually came from freshwater rivers and ponds. Carp, pike, eels, and trout were eaten. Seafood would spoil before it reached the table, unless you lived near the sea.

Anything that flew was considered suitable food, especially pigeons. Birds that we would now protect from harm, such as herons, storks, and larks, were also killed and eaten. Dovecotes were built in the gardens of large houses. The birds would gather there, build nests and breed, providing a source of food, particularly in very cold winters.

Fruit such as strawberries and cherries grew for a short time in the summer and did not stay fresh. Apples and pears were more common, as well as a type of cooking apple known as a pomewater. In the early 1600s, travelers from Spain and North Africa began to bring back oranges and lemons, but these fruits did not often reach people in the country. The climate in England was usually not hot enough to grow grapes, apricots, and peaches, though these were common in Europe. Figs, dates, and raisins were luxury **imports**.

What did people drink at this time? The dried leaf that is used to make tea and the roasted bean that produces coffee were still unknown in Europe. Instead, **ale**, which tasted like weak beer,

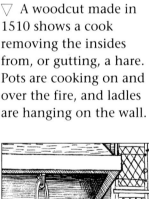

△ This 16th-century enameled dish shows a well-tended garden, full of a rich variety of fruits. Pomona, "the fair gardener," seems to be supervising the work rather than doing it herself.

▽ A woodcut made in 1510 shows a cook removing the insides from, or gutting, a hare. Pots are cooking on and over the fire, and ladles are hanging on the wall.

Sully, a minister at the court of Henri IV of France, wrote: "Tilling the land and tending the flocks are the two breasts from which France is fed."

was the usual drink for adults and children alike. Cider from apples, perry from pears, and mead from honey were also drunk. Wine was the drink at court and for the nobles and rich people. It was brought, or imported, to Britain from France and Spain, but it often tasted so bad that water or sugar was usually added.

People in the country did not eat breakfast. They usually ate two meals a day. Dinner was served at 11 A.M., and supper at 4 o'clock. In summer, haymakers and harvesters would take bread and an onion, with an apple, cake, or **pasty**, into the fields, together with ale or cider. In hard winters there was very little food, and there would be nothing fresh to eat. Poor people lived on thin soup, or **broth**, and dried peas.

A gentleman's life

A gentleman who lived in Normandy in France kept a journal of his life in the country from 1549 to 1563. His name was Gilles de Gouberville, and he gives a very good picture of what it was like to live a comfortable life. He grew apples and pears in his orchard and made cider and perry, as well as a strong drink we now call calvados. He kept bees, and a man would come to collect the honey, often also killing an animal for meat during his visit.

Because Gilles de Gouberville lived near the

▽ This scene of French country house life, from *Theatre de l'agriculture*, is by Olivier de Serres. You can see that food for the house came from the dovecote, the fish pond, the beehives, and the poultry yard.

An important book of the time gave information on farming and the cultivation of vegetables. It was called *Theatre de l'agriculture*, written by Olivier de Serres, and was first published in Paris in 1600. It contains many engravings showing the best way to farm successfully. In one picture you can see the master and mistress surveying their home. In the background, a gardener is pushing a wheelbarrow, and a workman is **threshing** corn. A dairymaid churns butter in her dairy, while hens, chickens, and pigs scavenge for food in the yard.

sea at Cherbourg, he often ate fresh fish. He also ate cabbage, beans, turnips, beets, peas, spinach, and lettuce. For meat, he had plenty of veal, **offal**, and black pudding. He also ate storks and fish called carp. The journal describes him sitting in his kitchen (where the animals were killed and cut up into joints of meat), doing his accounts and dozing in front of the fire.

△ This painting is called *A Man and a Woman before a Table Laid with Fruit and Vegetables*. There are peas and chestnuts, as well as the apples, pears, and cherries.

▷ This 16th-century picture shows olive oil being made. The olives are being poured into a vat (left) and then ground by a big stone. The oil was collected in jars or carried away in barrels.

Food in towns and cities

Life in towns and cities for most people in Tudor times was dirty and noisy. Disease was common. Rubbish and human waste, or **sewage**, were dumped straight into the rivers. In London there was a filthy stream, called the Fleet Ditch, that flowed into the Thames River. People had no idea that there was any link between illness and poor sanitation.

Most Tudor towns were very small compared with today's towns. In the London area of Chelsea, then deep in the country, crops were grown for sale. Houses in towns had their own "back-side," a small plot of garden, in which to grow vegetables or to keep a pig. In Manchester pigs hunted through rubbish in the streets for food. Many people ate a simple diet of boiled beef pottage, bread, and ale.

Staying in towns

Towns were the centers of trade and wealth. Traders and **merchants** bought and sold, and

▽ This 16th-century Dutch painting is by Lucas van Valkenbosch. It shows a woman with her children shopping for vegetables. You can see cabbages, cauliflowers, beans, and a cucumber. The red fruits in the baskets are cherries. In the background there is the marketplace, where people are looking at and buying fresh produce.

Henry VIII was a huge man who liked to eat well. In big cities he and other members of his court would often carry a piece of orange when they were out among the people. The king would hold the orange piece under his nose in order to mask the foul smells of streets and unwashed people.

△ Monks making wine at Saint-Germain-des-Près, Paris.

Many vineyards were destroyed in times of war. When the monks started to grow vines again, they hid the wine in cellars. The cold, dark conditions turned out to be ideal for storing the wine.

The dangers of gluttony

Olivier de Serres wrote in 1600: "When a gentleman attains an income of £500 [about $750], he no longer knows what it is to eat well, because, wishing to eat in the grand style, he eats in the *salle* [dining room] at the mercy of his cook, where previously he had taken his meals in the kitchen, having himself served according to his own tastes."

more and more goods were sent to other countries in exchange for gold and silver, herbs and spices, and new kinds of food.

In towns and cities, inns and **taverns** served a wide range of food to merchants and travelers. Drinking was often on a grand scale, and so was the drunkenness that followed it! Beer, ale, and cider, were served, as well as *clairet*, a light, clear, red wine that is now called claret. Darker, thicker red wines came from Spain, and port wine came from Portugal.

In schools and hospitals, as well as universities and inns of court (where lawyers were trained), dinner was served at noon and supper at 5 o'clock. Meals were expensive for visitors, but pupils and students could afford to eat quite well. Fruit, vegetables, eggs, and salad, with meat or fish served once a day, provided them with a good diet. People who could not make a living because they were old, poor, or sick went to live in the poorhouse. Poorhouse food was plain and simple: rye bread, porridge, cheese, salted herring, and beer.

Rich people could afford to eat plenty of meat. A country squire named William Darrell came to London from Wiltshire and was "detained by matters of law." He rented rooms and ate well. Joints of beef and mutton were served, along with side dishes of **game** (including rabbits, pigeons, and pheasants). He was served bread, butter, and cheese, with beer to drink. The main vegetable he ate was dried peas, which suggests it was winter. On Friday, he wrote, he was served carp, pike, and salted herring.

Town kitchens

We get a clear idea, from pictures and journals of the time, of how people ate in towns. Most kitchens did not have what

▽ This woodcut shows a bakeshop. Bread and pies are being cooked. Wooden logs are drying on the rack above the oven.

This kitchen scene shows a mass of fascinating detail. The artist, Floris van Schooten, has painted items of cooking equipment, as well as a full range of fruits—including melons, pomegranates, and gooseberries—and vegetables such as artichokes. There are also joints of pork, smoked fish, sausages, cheese, and larks.

we would call a stove. Instead, there was an open fire in a hearth. Food was cooked in large iron pots called **cauldrons**, which were hung over the fire. For feasts and special occasions, a whole animal such as a pig, ox, or even a deer would be skinned and put onto a spit. The meat was then turned around and around over the fire so that it cooked evenly and did not burn.

At tables in richer houses, trenchers were being replaced by plates made of **pewter**, silver, or pottery. These were better for holding the sauces and gravies that went with many dishes. For years, people had eaten with their fingers, cutting meat with a knife and scooping up broth with a spoon. The first forks had two prongs, or **tines**, and were used to serve food rather than to eat it with.

Some of the townspeople would eat and drink heavily at a feast to make up for weeks of a boring diet that consisted of broth, rye and barley bread, with ale. There would be music, dancing, bullbaiting, bearbaiting, and cockfights. At the end of the feast, some people would have "guzzled, and become cupshotten [drunk]."

In 1600 a French writer named Thomas Artus made fun of diners who were having difficulties using a fork for the first time. (At this time, people were not allowed even to touch the food with their hands.)

"They took it [the salad] with their forks . . . then they were served some artichokes, asparagus, peas, and shelled broad beans, and it was a delight to see them eating all this with their forks. For those who were not as nimble-fingered as the others, they dropped as much on their plates, the dishes, and all around, as they put in their mouths."

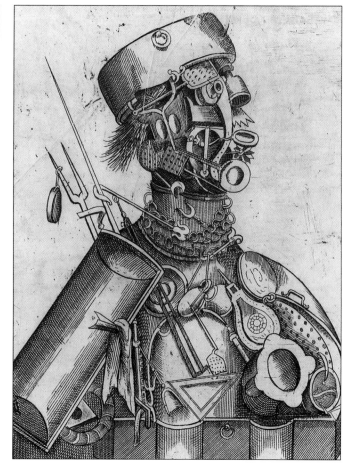

◁ A wooden engraving by Arcimboldo of kitchen equipment. Like the fruit and vegetables on page 5, the utensils have been put together to look like a very odd man: a fork, bellows, and a **mortar** are among the items.

▽ This 16th-century picture shows a kitchen scene. In his left hand, the cook holds a skimmer, which was used to skim off fat or unwanted pieces of food from the top of a cauldron. He is also holding a spoon and tasting the food.

Families ate together, and they all ate the same food. Children and women ate less than men, we are told, but everyone drank ale or watered-down wine. It was not safe to drink milk or water. Meat was banned on Fridays and during Lent (the forty days before Easter), when fish was served.

It is hard for us to imagine that the only way of making fresh food last was to cure it with salt or smoke. There was no **refrigeration**, although icehouses were built in big houses so that guests could add ice to their drinks. Food spoiled very quickly, and strong sauces and spices were used to cover up the awful tastes and smells.

Diet and health

◁ This engraving is "January" from *The Twelve Months* made by Etienne Delaune in 1568. It shows diners being served in a separate room while the cook works at an open fire in the kitchen. Wine is being poured, and you can see a trencher on the table. The dogs wait patiently for scraps of food.

No one knew much about which foods were good or bad for you. In the summer, fruit would sometimes overripen in the heat. Anyone who ate spoiled fruit got **diarrhea**, so people thought the fruit itself was the cause and could be bad for you.

People ate a lot of sweet things. This rotted their teeth and turned them black. Paintings of the time rarely show us this, but when Henry VII died in 1509, a description of him at the time read: ". . . small blue eyes, only a few

▷ In this woodcut, made by Hans Burgkmair in 1542, a cook is broiling fish and tasting the sauces that will go with it.

Shakespeare's play *King Henry IV*, *Part II* is about life in the time of King Henry IV (1399-1413). However, Shakespeare is really painting a picture of life at the time he wrote the play, which was first performed in 1597 or 1598. Master Shallow describes the food he would like William the cook to prepare for him:

"Some pigeons . . . a couple of short-legged hens, a joint of mutton and any pretty little tiny kickshaws . . ."

Kickshaws (from the French *quelques choses*, which means "some things") were small **delicacies**.

blackish teeth, thin white hair, and a pale face."

People in the 16th century thought that their health was governed by four "humors." They also believed that these four emotional states were affected by what they ate. So, depending on whether they were "sanguine" (steady), "phlegmatic" (calm and quiet), "choleric" (short-tempered and angry), or "melancholic" (sad and depressed), they needed to eat different kinds of foods—dry or moist, hot or cold.

Pasta made from flour and elaborate sugar **confectioneries** were new foods, while olives and grapes became more common. Gradually, people began to realize that simple food—fresh vegetables in salads, eggs, and fruit—were what people needed to stay well.

We have a good idea of what food was available in English cities at this time. French nobles, fleeing from the dangers of the **Wars of Religion** between Catholics and **Protestants** in France, were provided with a phrase book. This described the types of food and the dishes they would be likely to find on arrival in England. But the clearest picture of town and city life that we see shows filth, poverty, and disease.

▽ In this market, there is a rich selection of fruits, including cherries and grapes. The woman has artichokes in her basket. The men are perhaps travelers who have arrived in the city and are having a glass of wine while the women do the shopping.

Dishes served to French Huguenots

The Huguenots were French people who did not follow the teachings of the Catholic Church. They were Protestants.

- leg of mutton with garlic
- venison pasty with sugared mustard
- capon (chicken) and leeks
- blackbirds, larks, and partridges
- pike and carp
- hare and veal, as rare delicacies
- roasted apples and pears
- "scrapped" (small pieces of) cheese

Food for nobles and royals

In the 16th century, life at court became grander and the feasts were more extravagant. Although this was a way of living that only a tiny part of the population enjoyed, we have many records from the time—paintings, journals and diaries from visitors, and account books. The English royal court consisted of 1,200 courtiers in winter and about 800 in summer. (Many courtiers visited their homes, away from London, in the summer months.) This was a great many mouths to feed.

A royal kitchen

▽ A fete at Bermondsey, London, which was then in leafy countryside. Dancers, musicians, and the honored guests (far right) stand before a feast about to be served in the background.

Many of the Tudor royal palaces still stand, and some have been restored to show the kitchens and dining halls as they must have been at the time. Hampton Court, near London, was the home of Cardinal Wolsey until 1529, and then of his king, Henry VIII. Its kitchens are the largest and most complete in Europe.

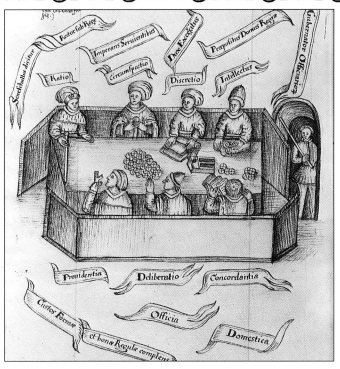

◁ The people who ran the kitchens and dining halls at Hampton Court were known as the Board of the Greencloth. The Latin words *ratio* (reason), *intellectus* (intelligence), and *discretio* (discretion) are all ways of encouraging the board to do its job well.

Rooms in the kitchens at Hampton Court

spicery	to store spices
chandlery	to store candles
flesh larder	where fresh meat such as deer or wild boar was kept
wet larder	where fish was kept fresh and cool in seaweed
bakery	where bread was made and baked
boiling house	held the cauldron for boiling and softening meat

The kitchen area at Hampton Court was built in 1514 and added to by Henry VIII. In it, three master cooks worked, helped by twelve assistants and seven galopins, (boys whose job it was to turn the spit). The boys were given ale to quench their thirst.

In the boiling house there was a large cauldron in which meat was boiled to soften it before making broth. It contained about 65 gallons. The bakery was built near the river's edge in case of fire. Fresh water was piped in from springs in Kingston, about 5 miles away. Rubbish, of course, went straight into the river.

Fine feasts

Royal feasts consisted of many dishes, but they were usually served as two courses. However, these courses were not like the single dishes at meals today. Instead, they were more like a buffet with a wide choice of dishes, both savory and sweet. Some were served in a *messe* (a dish for two or four people). This saved time as the servants rushed back and forth trying to attend to everyone.

A Spanish nobleman visiting Hampton Court for the first time describes the scene: "There are 18 kitchens going at full blast. They seem a veritable hell such is the stir and bustle in them." At the feast of St. John's Day, Midsummer's Day, June 24, 1542, we know that the following menu was served:

First Course
Cheat and manchet bread
Beer and ale
Wine
Chines of beef with vinegar sauce
Pestells [pies] of red deer
Baked carp in wine with prunes
Butter and eggs
Wafers

Second Course
Boiled mutton
Swan
Cocks
Roast boar with pudding
Cream of almonds
Wafers
Marchpanes

An Elizabethan feast in 1588

The food served included "joints of venison roasted in rye, sides of beef, boars' heads; bacon, brawn, calves' feet, ham, game pies with cinnamon; peacock, herons, blackbirds, larks; salmon, eels, turbot, whiting, sprats, oysters; sweetmeats, syrups, jellies, candied roses and violets, grapes, oranges, almonds, hazel nuts; cakes and sugar-soaked confections."

Food at feasts was often served in two sittings in order to fit in all the people. The king himself rarely attended these feasts. He had his own rooms in which food was served that had been cooked specially for him. Even when Queen Elizabeth attended a royal feast in 1588, she had someone to taste all her food before she ate it, in case an enemy had poisoned it.

Some of the dishes that were served at feasts in palaces were very elaborate. Swans and peacocks were cooked whole, and their beaks decorated with gold paint. There were also sugar shapes, sometimes spun like thread. These were known as subtleties, and were often made with marchpane (marzipan).

Vast quantities of ale and wine were drunk at feasts. At Hampton Court, 300 barrels of beer were consumed each year. Port and other wines from France, Spain, and Portugal were kept in cellars below the kitchens.

Royal shows

This was also a time of great competition between nations, especially old enemies such as France and Spain. Each wanted to outdo the other in terms of grandeur and the display of wealth. In 1520 Henry VIII and François I put

▽ This extravagant scene shows the Field of the Cloth of Gold outside Calais in 1520. On the far right, food is being served in a tent.

△ This Italian woodcut shows the main kitchen (*cucina principale*) in a big house. Note the plates on the table, the knives on the wall, and the joint of meat being roasted on the spit.

on a great show outside Calais. This was a form of royal showing off, known as the Field of the Cloth of Gold. Paintings of the event show an open-air feast being served in tents. Fortunately, it seems, the weather was good.

The French masked banquet, or masquerade, at Bayonne in 1565 was not so lucky. A pavilion was built on an island in the river. Horses were disguised as elephants, and boats were decorated to look like whales. Soldiers wore costumes to make them look like shepherdesses.

Unfortunately, a thunderstorm broke in the middle of the banquet. Rain poured down. The "whales" ran onto the banks, and the royal guests were drenched. However, the tapestry of the event made for the royal family of Valois shows the scene appearing to take place under a clear blue sky.

Royal travels

Tudor kings and queens moved around to meet their people. Traveling was difficult, so this could be done only in the summer.

Elizabeth I often ended her summer travels at Charlecote Park near Warwick. Here, open-air feasts and celebrations, including firework displays and concerts, took place.

In 1564 Catherine de Médicis, Queen of France, and her nine-year-old son, Charles IX, set off on a journey around France that lasted two years. A master cook and five assistants went with them. Local people who helped probably learned new ways of cooking from them.

▽ A royal picnic, perhaps at Charlecote Park. Queen Elizabeth I is being waited on, while members of her court sit on the ground and enjoy the food and drink.

Henry VII went on what he called a royal progress. He paid for some of his food—a shilling for beer, one shilling and eightpence for cherries and strawberries, and three shillings and fourpence for corn in someone's field (which his deer ate by mistake!).

Food for travelers

Travel over land in Europe in Tudor times was slow and difficult. A message could be sent from Edinburgh to London in three days, but only by using horses and changing them every 10 miles or so at **posthouses**. No good roads had been built since Roman times, more than 1,000 years earlier. In winter, rain caused floods and mud, while snow and ice could slow progress even more. Local people sometimes cut down trees or bushes blocking a road or filled in the biggest holes. Highway robbers were an ever-present danger.

Many rivers were no longer **navigable**, having silted up over the years. Only the estuaries that were also ports, such as Bristol and London, could take ships. It was quicker to send corn or wool from Wales to London by sea. Coal from Newcastle also reached London more quickly by sea than by land.

We are used to fresh food arriving quickly from all over the world, but in Tudor times food had to be grown and provided where it was needed. No one knew that keeping food frozen made it last longer. Salting, curing, and pickling were the common ways of preserving

▽ The cooks prepare the food for travelers at an inn while a guest waits patiently. The man on the left is probably the innkeeper. He may be carrying a lamp.

△ A Dutch merchant, visiting The Feathers Inn at Ludlow, in England, wrote: "The neat cleanliness, the pleasant and delightful furniture in every point for the household, wonderfully rejoiced me."

A phrase book used by French people traveling in England at the time advised the traveler to ask the chambermaid: "My she friend, is my bed made? Is it good? Pull off my hose [stockings], and warm my bed . . . I thank you, fair maiden."

▽ This Italian open-air kitchen shows all the equipment a traveling cook would need—cauldrons, spits, and cooking pots, as well as bowls and plates. The food was roasted on a spit or boiled.

food. For the traveler, food was a problem. It led to the setting up of inns and taverns on the main routes. Here travelers could change or feed their horses, eat a good meal, and spend a dry, warm night before continuing their journey. Many of these inns still stand and provide some of the same **hospitality**.

In spite of the difficulties, in Europe people began to travel more. This affected what they knew or could learn from other countries. Italy was now at the heart of learning and religion, the **Holy Roman Empire**. Catherine de Médicis, the Florentine bride of Henri II, came to France from Italy in the late 1590s. She (and others) brought changes to people's choices of food and to the way in which it was served.

Explorers and traders

While land travel was much the same as it had been for hundreds of years, there was a huge increase in sea travel during the 16th century. The main reason for this was the search for new trading routes and greater riches. The Spanish conquered Mexico and large parts of

A student's diary

A Swiss medical student, Felix Platter, traveled from Basel to Montpellier to study. His diary tells us about food and travel. For his last supper, before he left home, Platter's mother cooked him a quail he had kept as a pet. On his journeys he was constantly at risk from cheats, robbers, and bad food. At one inn he was even served with a pie made from cat meat.

In France, Platter lodged with a family who did not eat pork. Mutton was the usual meat, with plenty of cabbage and root vegetables. Platter got into trouble for eating eggs during Lent, which was forbidden. He tried olives and noted the arrival of cherries in spring, the onion fair at the end of August, and the wine harvest. After receiving his degree, he and other students paraded through the town carrying fennel stalks coated in sugar. To celebrate, they drank mulled wine made with herbs, called *hypocras*.

▷ *The Amerindian Town of Secoton in 1580*, by John White. Secoton was in what is now the state of Virginia. The maize on the right is, from the top, "rype [ripe]," "green," and "newly sprong [sprung]."

the Caribbean and South America, returning with gold, silver, and precious stones. Exploration led to settlement, or **colonization**. Ships returning to Europe with treasure were often attacked and their precious cargo stolen.

The voyagers brought back new foods from their travels. Herbs and spices that could not be grown in the colder European climate started to appear: ginger, nutmeg, peppers—and sugar. Potatoes, as well as tomatoes, are said to have come from North America. Sailors from Venice went to Mexico and exchanged grain for sugar cane. They brought back turkeys for the first time. Maize (or corn) was a new vegetable, although historians believe maize may have been grown in China and the Middle East.

Sailors who traveled on voyages of exploration or stole treasure from ships on the high seas had to spend many months away from land in terrible conditions. There was no fresh water. The ale and wine would turn sour, and the ship's hard biscuit would become full of

At the time of the explorers' arrival in America, a Navajo medicine man was recorded as saying: "Joy and beauty, may the sweet yellow maize accompany you to the end of the earth."

maggots. The dried meat and fish were so tough that they had to be boiled for a long time to soften them up. No one at the time understood the value of fresh fruit and vegetables, and many sailors died of **scurvy** and other diseases.

Writing about food

Many writers at the time complained about the huge amount of food eaten at banquets. They said that people would be harmed by mixing dishes and by eating too many rich sauces.

A French writer, François Rabelais, described an imaginary country ruled by a demanding king known as "Sir Belly." The people of this country were called "gastrolators," and they had to please Sir Belly by offering him food all the time. Rabelais's story of Sir Belly was, in fact, about France and the way people's eating habits were changing. These changes, which started in Tudor times, were to continue throughout Europe for both rich and poor people over the next couple of centuries.

▽ *An Old Woman Cooking Eggs*, by the Spanish painter Velázquez (1599-1660). The food is being cooked over a charcoal stove.

▽ This 16th-century feast has not been made to look more elegant than it really was! People are eating with their fingers and drinking out of mugs, while dogs sniff around the floor for bones and bits of meat.

Meals and recipes

Dinner at Sulgrave Manor, 1572

Venison pie with sugared mustard
Roast shoulder of veal
Roast leg of mutton stuffed with garlic, bread, and
cabbage

Trout, pickerels (young pike), and salted herrings

Capon (chicken) boiled with leeks
Pieces of roasted turkey-cock (turkey)
Roast partridge

Jelly, with candied flowers, gilliflowers (cloves),
and sugar paste

Sulgrave Manor was the Elizabethan home of the ancestors of George Washington. Life there was not as grand as in the royal palaces, or in a big house like Charlecote Park. But the family ate well, and the dishes served on special occasions such as the one above sound delicious. This dinner would have lasted for about three hours, with intervals in which the village fiddler played music for the family and guests.

Children and adults ate together. The father would first bless the food, and during the meal a toast in watered wine would be made to the monarch, the country, and the Washington family. At the end of the meal, a nursemaid would put the children to bed.

New foods

Explorers and travelers brought back many "new" foods to Europe during Tudor times. Today these foods are enjoyed all over the world. Trucks, trains, and planes can transport fresh produce quickly from one part of the world to another.

Tudor cooks relied on fresh food that was produced locally. They used more preserved foods in winter, when there was less fresh produce available. Food that is preserved by drying, salting, or pickling tastes different from preserved food today—which is usually canned or frozen. The meals you make will not taste the same as the ones served at Sulgrave Manor in Tudor times.

> **WARNING:** Sharp knives and boiling liquids are dangerous. Hot ovens and pans can burn you. *Always ask an adult to help you* when you are preparing or cooking food in the kitchen.

Pain Perdu – French Toast

Pain perdu means "lost bread" in French. This is a recipe to use up stale or leftover bread that would otherwise have been thrown away or "lost." Today we call this dish French toast.

Ingredients

4 large slices of whole-wheat *or* white bread

3 eggs

a pinch of salt

1/2 tsp cinnamon

1T butter

2T cooking oil

2 tsp confectioners' sugar

Ask an adult to help you when you start to cook.

1. Cut off the crusts from the bread. Take care to keep your fingers away from the blade of the knife.
2. Break the eggs into a small mixing bowl. Add the salt and cinnamon and whisk the mixture well.
3. Measure out the butter and put it in the frying pan. Measure out the oil and add it to the butter in the pan.
4. Pour the beaten egg mixture into a shallow dish.
5. Place the frying pan over a very low heat so that the butter melts. Stir the melted butter and oil together. Take care that the mixture does not burn.
6. Quickly dip the slices of bread in and out of the egg mixture. Make sure that both sides of each slice of bread are well covered with the egg mixture.
7. Transfer the bread to the frying pan and fry until golden brown on both sides.
8. Put the bread onto a serving dish *or* plates and sprinkle confectioners' sugar over each slice.

Equipment

bread knife

bread board

small mixing bowl

whisk

measuring cup

shallow dish

frying pan

spatula

serving dish *or* plates

teaspoon

Sharp knives, hot liquids, and hot pans are dangerous.

Chicken Blancmange

In Tudor times this light and tasty dish was served to people who were not well. A recipe for this dish was first printed in a 16th-century French cookbook.

Ingredients

1¼ cups water

1 chicken bouillon cube

1 lb chicken breasts

¼ tsp ground cardamom

½ tsp ground ginger

1 drop almond extract

6–8 peeled almonds

1 tsp confectioners' sugar

Equipment

measuring cup

large saucepan

wooden spoon

slotted spoon

food processor *or* meat grinder

large mixing bowl

fork

serving dish

Sharp knives, hot liquids, and hot pans are dangerous.

1. Measure out the water and pour it into a large saucepan. Bring the water to a boil and add the chicken bouillon cube. Stir the water until the bouillon cube has dissolved.
2. Ask an adult to take the skin off the chicken breasts for you. Then put the meat into the saucepan with the chicken bouillon.
3. Turn the heat down, so that the bouillon boils gently. Let the meat cook in the bouillon for about 30 minutes. Ask an adult to test the meat to make sure it is cooked.
4. Take the saucepan off the heat and allow the bouillon and meat to cool, for about 20 minutes. Use a slotted spoon to take the meat out of the saucepan.
5. Ask an adult to put the meat through a food processor *or* meat grinder for you, so that the meat is finely ground into a stiff paste.
6. Put the meat into a mixing bowl and add the cardamom, ginger, and almond extract. Mix everything together well with a fork. Gradually add about 3T of the chicken bouillon from the saucepan. The mixture should be stiff but not dry.
7. Spoon the mixture into a serving dish and smooth it down with the back of the spoon. Decorate the dish with almonds and sprinkle a little confectioners' sugar over the top.
8. If you are not going to eat the dish immediately, put it in the refrigerator and serve it chilled.

Fava Beans and Bacon

1. Put the fava beans in a large saucepan and cover them with cold water. Bring the water to a boil and then turn the heat down. Cook the beans for about 10 minutes, until they are tender.
2. When the beans are cooked, take the saucepan off the heat. Strain the beans and leave them in the colander to cool.
3. Carefully chop the parsley very fine, taking care to keep your fingers away from the knife blade.

Ingredients

1 lb shelled, fresh, *or* frozen fava beans

water

3 slices bacon

2T fresh parsley

2 tsp butter

¼ tsp salt

¼ tsp black pepper

Ask an adult to help you when you start to cook.

Equipment

large saucepan

colander

sharp knife

chopping board

large frying pan

spatula *or* wooden spoon

serving dish

Sharp knives, hot liquids, and hot pans are dangerous.

4. Carefully cut the bacon into small pieces with a sharp knife. Cut the butter into small pieces.

5. Put the butter in the frying pan and let it melt over a low heat. Then stir in the bacon pieces and turn up the heat a little.

6. When the bacon is almost cooked, add the fava beans, chopped parsley, black pepper, and salt.

7. Stir the mixture well so that the beans are covered with bacon and parsley. Then remove the frying pan from the heat.

8. Put the mixture in a dish and serve immediately.

"Roasted" Apples

In Tudor times these would have been roasted on a spit, in the same way as a turkey or a chicken. In this recipe the apples are "roasted" in the oven and could be served with roast pork or after roast turkey or a chicken.

1. Ask an adult to set the oven to 400°F.

2. Wash the apples and dry them. Ask an adult to core the apples for you and to make a slit in the skin with a sharp knife all the way around each apple's center.

3. Put the sugar, cinnamon, dates, and raisins in a mixing bowl and stir them well, until the fruit is well covered with sugar and cinnamon.

4. Stick a clove inside the top and the bottom of the hole that goes through the middle of each apple. Then stand the apples in the roasting pan.

5. Carefully stuff each apple with two dates and four raisins. Then fill up the hole in each apple with the sugar and cinnamon mixture.

6. Pour a tablespoon of water over the top of each apple so that there is a little water underneath each one.

7. Ask an adult to put the roasting pan into the oven for you. Let the apples cook for about 40 to 50 minutes.

8. Ask an adult to take the pan out of the oven for you and to put the apples on a serving dish. They can be eaten hot or cold.

Ingredients

4 large baking apples

4T dark brown sugar

2 tsp ground cinnamon

8 pitted dates

12–14 seedless raisins

8 cloves

4T water

Equipment

apple corer

sharp knife

mixing bowl

spoon

roasting pan

serving dish

Ask an adult to help you when you start to cook.

Glossary

ale: An alcoholic drink, like beer, usually made from hops, malt, water, and yeast. In Tudor times ale was made without hops.

banquet: A grand feast or public dinner.

brine: Salty water. Food stored in brine will keep well.

broadcasting: Scattering over a large area.

broth: A thin mixture of vegetables and water, drunk hot like a soup.

cauldron: A large pot, usually made of iron, for cooking over an open fire.

colonization: Rule by a government over another (or part of another) country.

confectionery: A sweet or pastry.

delicacy: A very small but tasty portion of food, which can be eaten in one mouthful.

diarrhea: A stomach upset that results in frequent and mainly liquid bowel movements to get rid of the waste matter.

dynasty: A series of rulers who are members of the same family. Also, the period of time during which several generations of the same family rule.

enclosed: Surrounded or fenced off.

famine: A time when people starve because there is not enough food.

feudal: Describes the way in that people held and worked the land for landowners during the Middle Ages. The feudal system slowly changed in Tudor times.

game: Animals, birds, and fish that are hunted for food and for sport.

harrow: A frame with spikes attached to it. It is pulled over the ground to break up the earth.

Holy Roman Empire: The empire in Western Europe that was founded in 962 A.D. and was based on the Roman Empire. It centered on what is now Germany and lasted for over 800 years.

hospitality: A friendly welcome given to visitors or guests. It usually includes the offer of meals and drinks.

import: Goods brought into one country from another.

manor: The area of land and property given to a noble by the ruler.

merchant: A person who buys and sells goods, often from other countries.

monarch: A ruler of a country—for example, a king, queen, or emperor.

mortar: A sturdy bowl or dish in which foods are ground into small pieces or powder, using a club or stick called a pestle.

navigable: Describes a stretch of water along which boats can sail or be steered.

offal: The parts of an animal cut out during butchering, such as kidneys, heart, lungs, stomach, or liver.

pasty:	A pastry "parcel," filled with a mixture of meat and vegetables.
pewter:	A metal made from a mixture of tin and lead, which was often used in Tudor times to make mugs, plates, and serving dishes.
posthouse:	A house where horses were kept for travelers. Traveling a long distance, and changing horses regularly, was called posting.
pottage:	A soup or stew, thickened with vegetables, lentils, or grains until it is almost solid, like porridge.
preserve:	To treat food or drink so that it would keep for a long time without spoiling.
Protestants:	People who belonged to one of the Christian churches that separated from the Church of Rome in the 16th century.
refrigeration:	The process of making, or keeping, something cold, usually to preserve it.
Renaissance:	This French word means "rebirth." It refers to the period in Europe, from the 14th to the 16th centuries, when there was a revival (rebirth) of interest in the arts and learning. The Renaissance was based on studies of ancient civilizations, particularly those of the Greeks and Romans.
scurvy:	A skin disease that people suffer from if they don't eat enough food that contains Vitamin C. This vitamin occurs mainly in fresh fruit and vegetables.
sewage:	Mainly liquid waste matter that is carried away from buildings through pipes, channels, or ditches.
spit:	A long, thin metal bar, often pointed at one end, that pierces food and holds it while the food is cooking.
stocks:	A heavy wooden framework made with holes and fastenings for the feet and arms. People were held in the stocks as a punishment. The stocks were in public places, such as the village square, so that everyone could see who was being punished.
tavern:	A place where ale, beer, and wine is sold and drunk. Taverns often serve hot meals as well.
threshing:	Separating grain from its stalk.
tines:	The prongs, teeth, or points of a fork or comb.
Wars of Religion:	The wars in France between Protestants and Roman Catholics which took place between 1559 and 1598.

Further reading

Frost, Abigail. *Elizabeth I.* North Bellmore, N.Y.: Marshall Cavendish, 1989.

Ross, Stewart. *Elizabethan Life.* North Pomfret, Vt.: Trafalgar, 1991.

Saraga, Jessica. *Tudor Monarchs.* North Pomfret, Vt.: Trafalgar, 1991.

Shakespeare's England. North Bellmore, N.Y.: Marshall Cavendish, 1990.

Index

NOV

1996